RICKERBY HINDS
Writer & Director

Rickerby Hinds is a native of Honduras who came to Los Angeles aged 13. He has an MFA in playwrighting from UCLA's School of Theater, Film and Television Production where he was twice awarded the Audrey Skirball-Kenis Award for Best Play. He is a Fulbright Fellow and a Professor of Playwriting in the Department of Theater Film & Digital Production at the University of California, Riverside, and the only tenured hip-hop theatre Professor in the country.

Hinds is one of the pioneers of Hip-Hop theater which has the ability to challenge conventional notions of the stage while embracing its history and traditions. His work draws on his multifaceted background to create theater that is simultaneously challenging, compelling and entertaining. His productions explore the human condition employing the aesthetics, as well as the performance instruments of hip-hop culture – MCing, hip-hop dance, beatboxing, graffiti (aerosol art), and DJ-ing.

His work has been developed by venues including the Latino Theater Company, The Mark Taper Forum, Bay Area Playwrights Festival, The Royal Court Theatre in London and The Oregon Shakespeare Festival (where he presented the first hip-hop Theater play in their history), and has toured to Romania, Poland, Austria, Hungary and Turkey, his native Honduras, and numerous venues throughout the US.

First published in the UK in 2026 by Aurora Metro Publications Ltd.

Based at Books on the Rise, 80 Hill Rise, Richmond, TW10 6UB UK

www.aurorametro.com   info@aurorametro.com

FB/AuroraMetroBooks X @aurorametro Instagram aurora_metro

Cover image by Erin Lamar

With many thanks to: Amie Brian

Printed in the UK by 4edge printers on sustainably resourced paper.

ISBNs: 978-1-910798-09-6 (print)

978-1-910798-10-2 (ebook)

DREAMSCAPE

A Play based on True Events

RICKERBY HINDS

AURORA METRO BOOKS

Jada Evelyn Ramsey and John 'Faahz' Merchant in *Dreamscape*.
Photo: Charisma Benitez & Gianna Cosenza.

DREAMSCAPE

Written and directed by Rickerby Hinds

Cast for performances at the Omnibus Theatre London February 2026

Myeisha Mills   Jada Evelyn Ramsey
Beatboxer & Coroner (Feb 10-22)   Josiah Alpher
                        (Feb 24-28) John 'Faahz' Merchant

US Cast
Myeisha Mills   Natali Micciche
Beatboxer & Coroner   John 'Faahz' Merchant

Producer   Andy Jordan
Choreographer   Carrie Mykuls
Lighting Designer & Production Manager   Chris Corner
Project Manager   Gabrielle Williams

Thanks to Tyisha Miller, Bernell Butler and the family for allowing us to tell this story.

Hindsight Productions is a Riverside, California—based creative content production company founded by award-winning playwright Rickerby Hinds. The company is dedicated to supporting creatives of color and producing bold, socially engaged work across film, theater, and interdisciplinary performance.

Their debut feature film, *My Name Is Myeisha*, received critical acclaim and multiple festival awards. Additional projects include *FOUR* (2025), *HA-YA!*, *Blackbox*, and *The Last Play* by Rickérby Hinds, a meta-theatrical exploration of art, identity, and legacy

BIOGRAPHIES

JOSIAH ALPHER

Josiah is an actor and digital creator from Northern California and a graduate of the University of California, Riverside, where he earned his B.A. in Theatre, Film, and Digital Production. His theatre credits include *Cabaret* (2022) and *Blackbox* by Rickerby Hinds (2023). On screen, his work includes *Four* (2025) and a series regular role on Brat TV's *Charmers* (2021). He looks forward to continuing to share stories that connect and inspire across stage, film, and television.

JADA EVELYN RAMSEY

Jada graduated from University of California, Riverside, in Theater, Film and Digital Production, where she was recognised with the Chancellor's Performance Awards

(2023/2024), a Gluck Film Fellowship Performance Award (2022) and a UCR Theater, Film, & Digital Award for Acting in a Leading Role. Her film work whilst training included *Four, Limbo Limbo, Surrender, Masked Despair and Magpie Maggie.* Theatre included *Blackbox* by Rickerby Hinds and *Men on Boats* by Jaclyn Backhaus. Inspired by her family, Jada is dedicated to telling stories that celebrate the strength and complexity of women who challenge societal norms and redefine expectations.

NATALI MICCICHE

Natali is an award-winning actor, dancer, and storyteller. Her work has earned the NAACP Theatre Award for Best Actress and received international acclaim at the Edinburgh Fringe Festival, where critics praised her physical poetry, emotional depth, and cultural resonance. Natali made her feature debut in *Coming to America 2* and also works behind the camera as a producer and director, creating bold, inclusive stories.

JOHN 'FAAHZ' MERCHANT

John is a multi-talented entertainer born and raised in Pomona, California. He discovered his voice, literally, at just six years old, when he began beatboxing and building the foundation for what would become a dynamic and versatile artistic career. Over the years, Faahz has evolved into an internationally acclaimed beatboxer, host, actor, and voiceover artist, captivating audiences with his creativity, charisma, and authentic storytelling. Driven by a deep passion for music, performance, and community, Faahz uses his platform to uplift and motivate youth around the world. His mission is to encourage young people to pursue education, follow their passions fearlessly, and embrace the transformative power of the arts. Whether on stage, on screen, or behind the mic, Faahz brings a message of resilience, growth, and global unity – leaving a lasting impact wherever he goes.

ANDY JORDAN PRODUCTIONS

An independent production company formed in 2000 with a focus on new writing, its 55 productions include: *Picasso's Women* (co-production with ATG and Assembly Theatre; EdFringe 2000, Assembly, then National Tour, starring Cherie Lunghi, Gwen Taylor, Jerry Hall, Toyah Willcox, Susannah York, 2000/2001); *Lies Have Been Told: An Evening With Robert Maxwell* (Pleasance Theatre, EdFringe, 2006, Trafalgar Studios, West End, 2006/2007); *A Midsummer Night's Madness* (AJP & Hackney Empire Theatre, EdFringe, CVenues, & Hackney Empire Theatre, London, Fresh Air Best Production Award, 2010); *Bette and Joan* (AJP & Ann Pinnington Productions, Arts Theatre, West End, starring Greta Scacchi, Anita Dobson, original music by Brian May of Queen, 2011); *September in the Rain,* written/directed by John Godber (AJP co-production with The Booking Office & Malvern Theatres, National Tour, starring John Thomson, Claire Sweeney, 2013); *Strindberg's Women* (AJP & Elysium Theatre Company, Jermyn Street Theatre, London, 2016), *Cops* (AJP & Pluto Productions, Southwark Playhouse, London, 2020); an ACE R&D workshop on *Hunt the Tiger* by Richard Vergette (Cast Theatre, Doncaster, 2020); *Hiya Dolly!* & *Leaving Vietnam* (EdFringe, 2022); *Leaving Vietnam* (Park Theatre, London, 2023); *The Shroud Maker* (Pleasance, EdFringe, 2024), *Lies Where It Falls, Born in the USA, Sinatra: RAW* (CArts, EdFringe 2024); *Lies Where It Falls* (Finborough Theatre, London, 2024); *Born in the USA* (National Tour, 2025/2026); *Dreamscape, Tilly No-Body* (Gilded Balloon, EdFringe, 2025); *Dreamscape* (59E59 Street Theaters & SoHo Playhouse, New York, 2026).

www.andyjordanproductions.co.uk

BIOGRAPHIES

ANDY JORDAN

Producer for Andy Jordan Productions

Andy Jordan is an award winning Producer and Director, working in theater, audio and online drama. He is well known for discovering and helping develop new writers for theater, TV, radio and film, many of whomare now internationally recognized including Jimmy McGovern and Richard Bean. He founded one of the first national touring new writing companies, Bristol Express. His directing credits include work in the West End, Off-West End, EdFringe, UK regional theatres, and productions in New York, Warsaw, Hong Kong, Paris and San Francisco. Recent theatre directing credits include *The Inn at Lydda* (Shakespeare's Globe Theatre, London) and *Born in the USA* (EdFringe & Park Theatre, London). He was a Senior Radio Drama Producer at the BBC, producing many award-winning productions. He now regularly makes BBC audio dramas from the independent sector, including an adaptation of *The Signalman* by Charles Dickens, starring James Purefoy, and *Jubilee!* by Garth Bardsley and Ray Shell, starring Samuel West and Simon Callow. He is also a Sound Artist, with recent exhibition and installation work including *Spellbound* (Ashmoleon Museum, Oxford). He has had a decades-long relationship with the Edinburgh Festival Fringe, having presented over 30 seasons of productions at EdFringe, including *Dreamscape* in 2025.

CHRIS CORNER

Production Manager for Andy Jordan Productions

As a freelance General & Production Manager, Chris has managed projects for many of the leading UK new writing companies including Foco Novo, Joint Stock, Bristol Express, Paines Plough, Bright Red, Moving Theatre, Lifeblood and Kali. He has also worked for for Leicester Haymarket, Sheffield Crucible, Royal Court and the Royal Opera House.He was Production Manager for National Early Music Festival for over 10 years. In 2017 he was General Manager of a production of *Troilus and Cressida* in Kyiv in which the Greek characters spoke Ukrainian and the invading Romans spoke Russian.

PREFACE

I view hip hop theater as one of the most potent artistic expressions of our time — both politically urgent and culturally transformative. Rooted in the language, movement, rhythm, and aesthetics of hip hop culture, it gives voice to marginalized communities, disrupts traditional theatrical forms, and reclaims space within institutions that have historically excluded Black and brown narratives. Hip hop Theater interrogates systems of power, exposes injustice, and amplifies lived experiences that are often silenced. It bridges generations, geographies and struggles —making it a vital platform for civic dialogue and cultural revolution.

After the death of Tyisha Miller, a 19-year-old African American woman shot and killed by city of Riverside police officers in the Inland Empire of Southern California, I was torn between trying to say something through my writing and wondering if it would appear that I was rushing to capitalize on another tragic event in the Black community. So, in spite of being aware and connected to the tragedy from the beginning, it wasn't until five years later that I decided I had to do something, to say something — not just about that situation but about the precarious balancing act that is the relationship between the Black community and the law, as embodied by the police in this situation.

The journey from decision to development of *Dreamscape* was a difficult one to say the least because my attempt to have words come out of the mouth of a 19 year-old young woman as she is being shot to death by the very police officers summoned to help her constantly took me to that same place of helplessness where she must have undoubtedly spent her last moments on this earth. It is a place African Americans have been forced to occupy when interacting with the enforcers of laws which were, for a time in our history, explicitly designed for our oppression and abuse and which now serve a more subtle purpose and space in our oppression, a place where arguments are now made to justify the millions of Black men and increasing number of Black women living under the law in prisons, or under the law outside prison walls.

– Rickerby Hinds

Jada Evelyn Ramsey, Josiah Alpher, John 'Faahz' Merchant and Natali Micciche in productions of *Dreamscape*.
Photo: Charisma Benitez, Gianna Cosenza, Gabrielle Williams
Composite: Luke Wakeman

DREAMSCAPE

Rickerby Hinds

Dreamscape received a record six 2016 Los Angeles NAACP nominations and won: Best Director, Best Lead Actor, Best Lead Actress. It has also been adapted into the award-winning film *My Name is Myeisha* which Rickerby Hinds co-wrote and produced.

The play had its UK premiere at Gilded Balloon as part of the Edinburgh Festival Fringe on 30 July 2025.

The play had its New York premiere at 59E59 Street Theaters on 7 January 2026.

The play had its London premiere at the Omnibus Theatre on 10 February 2026.

CHARACTERS

MYEISHA MILLS – 19, Female, African American

THE DJ/BEATBOXER – also 911 Dispatcher, Coroner, Officer Garland

The Time:
December 28th, 1998

PROLOGUE

Otis Redding's White Christmas gently disquiets the darkness. Chalk outlines of MYEISHA MILLS materialize. Lights rise to reveal MYEISHA rising from the front seat of her aunt's Nissan Sentra. She dances the Twelve Mortal Moves *as the music is spasmodically disrupted by twelve distortions - these are gun shots — each one finds its target in MYEISHA's body, transforming her movement into a dazzling life-death-dance. She lands in the front seat of the car, closes her eyes for a moment then awakens with a jolt.*

MYEISHA *(frightened)* Ever have one of those dreams
Where nothing comes out when you try to scream?

(Commanding herself)

Scream
Screeam!

She tries to scream but only a series of sampled "Hollas and Scream" are heard.
See what I mean?

One of *those* dreams

Christmas was three days ago
Jingle Bells and ho, ho, ho

Just so you know
This ain't gon be one of them feel-good shows
Just so you know

So
Christmas was three days ago
Jingle Bells and ho-oh, ho-oh, ho-oh *(as in somebody
sayin' ho-oh)*
Today's December 28th
Third day of Kwanzaa
Ujima
"To build and maintain our community together
And to make our brothers' and sisters' problems our
problems
And to solve them together"

I know you didn't know
I didn't know till uncle Darnell told me so during one of
his "black-outs"
Oh no, not that kind a black-out
That's just what we call it when uncle D has one of his
moments
And is compelled to bust you out 'cause of your lack of
blackness
You'll see what I mean

It's Ujima though

(Proudly) Umoja, Kujichagulia, Ujima

So

Me, Shy and my cousin Toni dying to get our party on
Rollin to L. A. though

Tired of Club Metro
Oh
For those of you who don't know me
See, I was born and raised in the I-E
That's the Inland Empire, the I-E
Sixty miles east of the City of Angels
Four dance floors of Hip Hop, Reggae, *(her least favorite) Rock en Español* and Retro
So
The Sentra starts to rattle and pull to the right
Ah man, I cannot believe we got a flat in the middle of the night
Not tonight

(At audience)

Okay, let's just let me get the facts folks
What is the deal with automobiles and (my) Black folks
Fo real
And the fact that your spare is always flat, folks
Fo real
And do not get me started on a working jack, folks

(my) Black folks

So I wind up in a fix at the Spirit of 76 that sits on Central'n Brockton
Gat in my lap case I get rocked-on
Waiting for Shy and Toni to get back with the Tripple-A card
One in the morning sittin in my aunt Gwen's ride

I can't leave aunt Gwen's Sentra sittin on Central
If it gets stolen scratched towed or broken into
Soon as I see her I'm-a be the one get broken in two
Aunt Gwen gon' kill me
Well, maybe not kill
But I sho' ain't gon' be rollin the Sentra no more
Feel

Ever have one of those dreams
Where nothing comes out when you (try to) scream
Tap

So I'm sitting in the Sentra on Central sensing
something soundin like rappin like tappin
Like...
(Singin With DJ/BEATBOXER)
Who's that peepin in my window
Sha-pow nobody now

(Spoken) Tap

I hear the tappin again
Oh cool it's Toni
Let me let you in, girl where you been? I'm lonely
Got me sittin at this station in the middle of the night
One in the morning loosing patience
Some'n some'n just ain't right

Tap

(To audience)
Now before you trip
Let me go on and admit that...
I'm strapped

Yeah, that's right
I'm strapped
(Slowly starting to rhyme)
With my gat at Central'n Brockt-on
Thirty-Eight in my lap case I get rocked-on

Yo that's nice
(Spittin with skillz this time)
So I'm strapped with my gat at Central'n Brockt-on
Thirty-Eight in my lap case I get rocked-on
Late at night in my lap there it sat
there I sat
there it sat
there I sat
there it sat
there I sat
Took a nap
Rat-ta-tat-tat-tat
Tap
Tap
Tap

I put the gat in my lap 'cause I was a little terrified

Ta-ta-ta-tappin' on the window cousin Toni outside
So I say "hold on cuz, let me let you in"
But 'fore I can
Here comes that damn dream again
(Tries to open door but can't move)
First I can't holla
Now I can't even move

Tryin' to open the door but I can't even move
Can't take this much more cause I can't even move
Feel like a prisoner of war and I can't even move
Can't move can't move can't move can't move
First I can't holla, now I can't even move
(To self) If you're dreamin Myeisha, girl wake up now fool!
(She sees TONI walking away from car)
Who you callin' this late on a pay phone
You better come on so we can get on and head on
Home
Toni, where are you goin' to?
Where the heck you been?
I'm opening the door least I'm tryin' to
Let me let you in
I know you're ready to go home girl, I'm dying to
We'll just explain it all to aunt Gwen
You can just explain it all to aunt Gwen
I'll just explain it all to aunt Gwen
We ain't fixin' no flat tonight forget that
Aunt Gwen's just gonna have to "get Black"

We ain't fixin' no flat tonight forget that
Aunt Gwen's just gonna have to "get Black."

Public Enemy's 911 Is A Joke *drops.*

DJ/BEATBOXER is DISPATCHER. MYEISHA is TONI.

1.

MYEISHA becomes TONI who picks up the pay phone and dials 911.

DISPATCHER 9-1-1.

TONI Yes uh, could you guys come down to uhm, Central and Brockton to the 76 gas station because there's a uhm, my cousin's in a car and she has a gun on her, but she's passed out. We can't get in the car 'cause it's locked.

DISPATCHER Okay, who's inside the car?

TONI Uh, my cousin.

DISPATCHER And she has a gun with her?

TONI Yes. It's sitting in her lap and uh, she's passed out.

DISPATCHER She's passed out?

TONI She's passed out.

DISPATCHER She has been drinking?

TONI I don't know. We just came--

DISPATCHER Do you think she shot herself?

TONI Yeah, she has a flat. I don't know.

DISPATCHER Okay. What kind of car is she in?

TONI It's a Nissan Sentra.

DISPATCHER Hold on. What color?

TONI White.

DISPATCHER Is she in a passenger or...

TONI She was drive... she was driving. 'Cause we came to fix, she had a flat tire. We came to help her fix it and uhm, and we just found her like this.

DISPATCHER Okay so she's in the car by herself.

TONI By herself.

DISPATCHER Have you tried to bang on the doors?

TONI Yeah, we banged on the window and everything. She's passed out. We cannot get her to wake up. The music is loud, so we can't do nothing.

DISPATCHER Okay. I'm gonna keep you on the phone until the officers are on their way. Okay?

OFFICER GARLAND On December 28, 1998, I was working the graveyard shift when I received a call from RPD Dispatch at approximately Oh-One-fifty-five hours assigning me to proceed to the point of origin of a 911 call which was Baines 76 Unocal gas station, located at 6575 Brockton Avenue in the City of Riverside. The call conveyed that there was an unresponsive female locked in a white Nissan Sentra with a visible firearm on her lap.

MYEISHA *(Rappin')* So I'm strapped with my gat at Central'n Brockt-on

Thirty-Eight in my lap case I get rocked-on

OFFICER GARLAND At approximately zero-two-hundred hours, I arrived on the scene and spoke with two females standing by the pay phone on the north side of the gas station's premises. The two females advised me that the female in the locked vehicle was a family member, that she appeared to be unconscious, and that she had a loaded firearm on her lap. I saw that the two females were very upset.

DISPATCHER She been--I'm sorry--has she been drinking today?

TONI I don't, I don't know! That's what I'm telling you. I don't know. She had a flat tire and she called the house. So we're coming back to give her the Triple A card--

DISPATCHER Uh-huh.

TONI ...so she can get the tire fixed. But this is how we found her. So we don't know.

DISPATCHER You don't know what's going on.

TONI Uh-uh.

OFFICER GARLAND Based on their demeanor and the occupant's non-responsiveness to her family members, I believed that the vehicle's occupant was necessarily in some sort of medical distress especially because her family members did not know what was wrong with her.

DISPATCHER How long ago did she, did you talk to her?

TONI Uhm, I didn't talk to her. My aunt did.

DISPATCHER How long ago was that?

TONI That was like 20 or 30 minutes ago.

Can you guys, can you guys send an ambulance with you?

DISPATCHER Yeah.

TONI Okay.

DISPATCHER Yeah, since we don't actually know what's wrong with her--

TONI Uh-huh?

DISPATCHER And... the gun, you can just see the gun?

TONI Yes. It's in her lap.

DISPATCHER It's sitting in her lap?

TONI Uh-huh.

DISPATCHER Okay. And she's the only one in the vehicle?

TONI Yes.

(Pause)

DISPATCHER What is her name?

MYEISHA My name is Myeisha

Y'all know us E-shas: Myeisha, Moesha, Aisha, La'Resha, La'Creesha, Ta'Nesha, Tyisha

We the E-shas we the first cousins to the Aw-nas

You know the Aw-nas: LaJuana, Tiana, Shawana, Juwanna, Tawanna.

DISPATCHER How old is she?

TONI Uhm, she's 19.

DISPATCHER Nineteen years old?

TONI Uh-huh.

DISPATCHER Okay. And the car is just parked in the, in a parking lot?

TONI Yeah, at the gas station.

DISPATCHER And when she called you twenty minutes ago she did, said she was alone?

TONI Uh, I don't know.

DISPATCHER Oh she never did...

TONI 'Cause my aunt talked to her so I don't--

DISPATCHER Okay.

TONI --I don't know.

OFFICER GARLAND As I finished speaking with the two witnesses, Officer Hobart arrived on the scene. I informed Officer Hobart that the vehicle's occupant was apparently unconscious and had a gun. Because the occupant had a gun, I knew that we would have to secure the area and make it safe for emergency medical personnel to render any aid the occupant required.

TONI How far is the uhm, police station from here?

DISPATCHER Well they're just, they're in the city just driving around--

TONI Oh.

DISPATCHER --But they're on their way there.

OFFICER GARLAND Officer Hobart and I approached the vehicle with our guns drawn and pointed downward.

TONI Oh.

DISPATCHER They don't sit at a police station, waiting...

TONI Okay, here... I see one police officer. They found the, uh, the car right now. There's a police car right now.

OFFICER GARLAND Officer Hobart approached along the passenger's side rear door as I approached along the driver's side door. From my position behind the driver's side rear door, I could see that the occupant's gun was on her lap pointed toward the driver's door.

DISPATCHER Okay. If they're coming—

TONI In the drive--

OFFICER GARLAND The gun's magazine was in place and the weapon was readily accessible.

DISPATCHER They're coming toward you?

OFFICER GARLAND After Officer Hobart and I verified the occupant had a gun...

TONI Yes.

OFFICER GARLAND I held that position until backup arrived.

DISPATCHER Why don't you go talk to 'em?

TONI Okay, thank you.

MYEISHA Soon's I hear the cops' sirens the first thing pop in my mind

"Man I wish I was a white girl" or at least a little lighter than I'm

Not white in the "I can flip my hair" and "I got blue eyes" kind-a way

But in the "Officer, can you help me out" kind-a way

In the "Young lady are you okay? You look distressed" kind-a way

In the "Are you okay, you need a ride? You look lost" kind-a way

But not today

Tonight my name's Myeisha... and I am Black... might-a had a little to drink

Those are just the facts

But even still with all that I figure I should still be alright

I mean if Toni couldn't hear me I must be asleep, right

And if I'm sleepin' I'm dreamin' so it must be deep, right

And if I'm sleep and it's deep-then the police'll wake me up, right

Show a little care, help me find a spare, even help jack me up, right

(pointing out writing on Police Unit)

To Protect and to Serve

Written in black and white

Right?

OFFICER GARLAND   I observed that the occupant appeared to be in dire medical distress and in need of immediate medical assistance. I observed that the occupant's mouth was slightly open, her eyes were closed, her breathing appeared shallow, her lips were quivering, her body was shaking, and a white substance was accumulating around the sides of her mouth.

Based on my prior experience with persons overdosing on drugs, I believed Mills was experiencing many symptoms which were consistent with a drug overdose. Believing that time was of the essence, I thought we should use the quickest means available to remove the gun from her presence so that medical personnel could render the necessary aid.

I would attempt to break the window and retrieve the gun.

MYEISHA interrupts OFFICER GARLAND. The DJ/ BEATBOXER is OFFICER GARLAND.

MYEISHA *(Rapping)* So I'm strapped with my gat at Central'n Brockt-on

Thirty-Eight in my lap case I get rocked-on

OFFICER GARLAND After verifying all the officers were in position, I performed a silent three count and then broke the window on my first attempt using the A-S-P baton. I then dropped the baton and leaned to tuck my body into the front window and grab the occupant's gun. As I reached in to retrieve the weapon, I heard a "boom" which I believed to be a gun shot go off toward my right ear.

MYEISHA *(Rappin')* So I'm strapped with my gat at Central'n Brockt-on

Thirty-Eight in my lap case I get rocked-on

OFFICER GARLAND Once I was inside the vehicle, I could no longer see the weapon

I thought that the occupant had grabbed her weapon and shot me

Once inside the vehicle I heard a boom which I believed to be a gun blast

Once inside the vehicle I heard a boom which I believed to be a gun blast

Once inside the vehicle I heard--

MYEISHA   *(Singing)* Happy birthday to you
Happy birthday to you
Happy birthday dear officer
Happy birthday to you

(About OFFICER GARLAND on floor of the Sentra)

Officer Garland, the one on the floor
It's his birthday today he's turning 24

(Singing Stevie Wonder's Happy Birthday)

Happy birthday to ya
Happy birthday to ya
Happy birthday
Happy birthday to ya
Happy birthday to ya
Happy birthday
Happy birth--

You see the problem with this version
Nobody knows how to end the thing

Happy birthday
Happy birthday to ya...

Yo wait
December twenty-eight
That would make the officer a Capricorn

Capricorns are supposed to be
Practical and prudent

Ambitious and disciplined
Careful and patient
Humorous and reserved
Pessimistic and fatalistic
December 28th

That makes officer Garland a Kwanzaa baby
Ujima baby
(Not really)
Well, maybe

December twenty-eight 1998
Means Y-2-K's only a year away
You heard of Y-2-K
Your ain't heard of Y-2-K?
Okay
They say one second after twelve next new year's eve
After they drop the ball on New York right
Things are gonna go bananas, fo real
End of the world
(They) say all the computers in the world are gonna lose their "magabites"
Like even banks and stuff are gonna lose grip on their cash

Of course nobody I know is so naive to believe
That some ATM's are gonna go crazy and start spittin out twenties
(*Still not convinced*)
I ain't sayin' I believe and I ain't sayin I don't

But... you know... me, Toni and Shy got the ATM on
University and Main staked out
We just gon' be in the vicinity case cash starts to spit
out
Think I won't?

But a thousand years
That's crazy to even try to think
A thousand years of time
If we're lucky we get like seventy-nine
That's like a blink
Like a wink

But at least I get to be one of the very few
In the history of the world to go from the old millennium
to the new
Out of everybody in history to ever live
I get to be one of the ones who gets to go through from
millennium one to millennium two

(At audience)

You too
Know what I'm gonna do
I'm gonna make the millennium that's next
My best
I'm-a make M-two tha bomb
Might even make me an M-two resolution
Start me an M-two revolution

December 28 Y-2-K in a year
Makes officer Garland a Capricorn over there

*DJ/BEATBOXER drops What's Your Sign cut. MYEISHA
gets audience hype.*

Let's see what other signs we got in the house tonight
(To audience)
Say what's your sign!?
Say what's your sign!?

Do the Pisces run this motha for ya?

Do the Aries run this motha for ya?

Do the Libras run this motha for ya?

Do the Taurus run this motha for ya?

December 28th Y-2-K in a year
Makes officer Garland a Capricorn over there

OFFICER GARLAND Once inside the vehicle I heard a
boom which I believed to be a gun blast. I immediately
fell backwards onto the pavement, injuring my legs
and wrists. I saw the occupant rise forward in her seat.
While still thinking that I had been shot and believing
that the occupant was attempting to shoot me again I
began firing into the driver's side door of the vehicle.

MYEISHA *(Convincing herself)* I mean if Toni couldn't
hear me I must be sleep, right?

OFFICER GARLAND I began firing into the driver's
side door of the vehicle

MYEISHA And if I'm sleep and I'm dreamin' it must be
deep, right?

OFFICER GARLAND I began firing into the driver's side...

MYEISHA And if I'm deep asleep the police'll just wake me up, right?

OFFICER GARLAND I began firing into the driver...

MYEISHA Help me find a spare, even help jack me up, right?

OFFICER GARLAND I began firing

MYEISHA Right?

OFFICER GARLAND I began firing

MYEISHA Right?

OFFICER GARLAND I began firing

MYEISHA Right?

OFFICER GARLAND I began firing

MYEISHA Right?

(Beat.)

Ever have one of those dreams

Where nothing comes out when you scream

She tries to scream. Nothing comes out. DJ/BEATBOXER samples a series of "ones" which mix into the music for MYEISHA's routine in next scene.

2.

MYEISHA is working on dance routine. As the CORONER "cuts up" the following, its effects are manifested in her dance.

CORONER The entrance to gunshot number one is located on the right upper arm.

This is a typical distant gunshot wound entrance. The course of the projectile is through the skin and soft tissue of the right arm, and perforating and fracturing the right humerus.

This is a serious, however, non-fatal gunshot wound to the right arm, fracturing the right humerus.

MYEISHA Did he/she say humorous I think he/she said humorous

DJ/BEATBOXER samples a series "humorous".

That's funny

What's [not so funny] no joke is the fact that me, Shy and Toni

Been workin' on our routine, you know, for when we hit the scene

(Mildly defensive)

Yeah, that's right, we them girls, you know the ones

Get you out on the dance floor thinkin' you gon have you some fun

Thinkin' you gon' get your freak on... your grind on... maybe even get you some

But as soon as we get you on the floor you realize you gets none

We [break out in our] bust out the routine we came here to do

Now we ain't tryin' to be mean, it's just how we do what
we do

So you end up standing there bobbin' your head
wondering if you're gonna get some attention... create
a little tension

So when we see it in your face we give you a little taste,
know what I mean

What you don't realize is that it's all built into the
routine

Did I mention

*DJ/BEATBOXER samples: Shai's Shy, Tony Toni Tone's
Tony, Toni Tone has done it again and Another Bad
Creations' Iesha,. MYEISHA become TONY, SHY and
then MYEISHA again on cue with the DJ/BEATBOXER's
samples.*

Like I said

We ain't mean, that's just how we play

We're Tony, Shy, Myeisha

We're three tha hard way!

So anyway, we workin' on a new routine the old one's
gettin' tired

Bout time for it to be retired

So...

Dances. Stops in the middle of humerus move.

See the dilemma?

This is where we're supposed to hit this

Tries "humerus" move again.

It's cool an' all

Me myself personally

I think we should be doing more of Aaliyah's moves

Girl is bad... and so smooth

She's got that thing, you know

She should do some more movies or something, you know

I bet you she's gonna really blow up in a couple years or so

But I get the feeling she might wanna give the slip to R. Kelly

Maybe it's just me but he gives me the (willies)

(Does "he gives me the willies" shake)

Anyway, check out what we got so far on the routine down

Then you'll see why a fractured humerus is not such a funny bone

MYEISHA dances routine, but can't hit the "humerus move". She notices that the CORONER cuts the record every time she gets to that move. She battles CORONER with the "humerus move" for control of the turntables, MYEISHA wins this battle.

MYEISHA then dances the routine, struggling through the "humerus" part. Frustrated, she makes her way back to the front seat of the Nissan Sentra where she finishes the routine.

3.

DJ/BEATBOXER samples a series of "Twos." MYEISHA dances the "fractured jaw move" as the CORONER "cuts up" the following.

CORONER The entrance to gunshot number two is located on the left posterior upper neck.

This is a typical distant gunshot wound entrance.

The course of the projectile is through the skin and soft tissue of the left upper neck, and coursing through the mandible and exiting the right side of the jaw.

The mandible is extensively fractured and there is some fragmentation of the teeth.

The exit to gunshot wound number two is on the right side of the jaw.

This is a very serious, however, not rapidly fatal gunshot wound, fracturing the jaw.

MYEISHA I heard that

Dreams about losing your teeth symbolize the loss of childhood innocence.

These dreams often occur at times of transition from one life stage to the next and can be a message that an important milestone is occurring and urging you to face the inevitable.

You know what I'm gonna miss

Graham's Mission Bar-B-Que

Downtown on Main street

Robert be puttin' his foot in his Q

Both feet

Oh, don't worry, that's a good thing, it's the same as sayin' mmm-mmuh!

That Q's slammin'

Beef tips

Cole Slaw

Mac and Cheese

Chicken

That's what I'm a be missin

Pork ribs

Potato salad

Bar-B-Que beans

Greens

Yams

Peach Cobbler

I got something that needs to be said though

So, what's the deal with our Bar-B-Que folks and their bread

Y'all heard what I said

The bread

The bread

If you can call it that

It's the same no matter where you're at

You can be at Graham's, Bobby Ray's in San Berdoo,
Louisiana Fish in Mo-Val or M&M's in L.A.

Your meal's gonna come out the same way

Greens gonna be hooked, Mac and Cheese... pleeeease

Baked beans gon be lip-smakin

And the Que's gonna be slammin

But sittin' on top of your order, off to the side

I guarantee there's gonna be some paper-thin, no flavor
it-ain't-even-Roman-Meal white bread

You heard what I said

White bread

I'm tellin you it's gonna be white

White bread

But if you accidently luck out and get some wheat
bread

Don't be lookin' for no wheat grains, wheat smell,
wheat germ or wheat taste

Nothin' like that found in this bread

This wheat bread is gonna be wheat only because that's
what the bag said

What's really sad is that since the rest of the meal's so
good

We forget about the bread white or wheat

And when it's time to sop up that last bit of Q sauce
out of the corners of that take-out Styrofoam container

that you can't reach with your plastic fork

That paper-thin, flavorless, you-wish-it was-Roman-Meal-bread gets it done

That's what I'm-a be missin

Bar-B-Que

Fake wheat bread

And

Kissin

Listen

Kissin

Okay

Wesley Snipes in *Sugar Hill* or Denzel in *Crimson Tide*

Okay

Denzel in *Hurricane* or Wesley Snipes in *White Men Can't Jump*

Okay

Wesley Snipes in *Murder at 1600* or Denzel in *Devil In A Blue Dress*

Okay

Denzel in *Glory* or Wesley in *Blade*

Okay

Wesley in *Blade II* or Denzel in *The Preacher's Wife*

Okay

Denzel in *Malcolm X* or Wesley in *Jungle Fever*

Okay

Wesley in *Blade III* or Denzel in *Training Day*

Okay

Denzel in *Mo' Betta Blues* or Wesley in *Mo' Betta Blues*

I heard that dreams about losing your teeth symbolize the loss of childhood innocence These dreams often occur at times of transition from one life stage to the next.

MYEISHA dances, but can't hit the "fractured jaw move". She notices that the CORONER cuts the record every time she gets to that move.

She battles CORONER with the "fractured jaw move" for control of the turntables trying to stop the him/her from cutting the record then letting it play.

MYEISHA wins this battle.

4.

DJ/BEATBOXER samples a series of "threes". MYEISHA dances the "right shoulder move" as the CORONER "cuts up" the following.

CORONER The entrance to gunshot number three is located on the right posterior shoulder on the right upper back.

The course of the projectile is through the right posterior shoulder and through the wall of the back.

This is a nonfatal distant gunshot wound to the back.

MYEISHA I was always a tomboy

People used to say I must be gay 'cause I dressed this way

Baggy jeans, sneakers and my shirt hangin loose this way

Always a tomboy and if you don't like it you can kiss this... this way

Looked good playin' the field

And still had sex appeal

Played some basketball, but softball was my game

Got my pitch up to 65 my last year at Riverside High even got a little fame

It's true

Got my picture in the Black Voice
News paper page B-2

My best pitch was the Quick-an'-Split

Had batters singin the blues

See-ya!

Loved the sound of my pitch in the catcher's met when it hit the sweet spot

It's like, like

(Omit following line if MYEISHA can pop gum inside mouth, just do it.) [like poppin' gum inside your mouth hittin' that perfect pop]

It sounded good,

Felt good

And I look good

Okay, let me stop

I did look good though

On the pitcher's mound MYEISHA strikes her left hand with her right as if wearing baseball glove. Blows a bubble, winds up and pitches. We hear the pop. It's the gum/its the ball in glove.

I'm thinkin bout walkin on at Cal State, or U.C.R., RCC, Valley or Cal Poly

I messed up and didn't get my applications in on time

(She pitches. Pops gum. self-congratulatory.)

Tomboy

Shoot, I could-a been a cheerleader if I wanted to

Homeboy

(Cheerleader style) My name's My-e-sha

I am the best

Come get with me

Forget the rest......

My name's My-e-sha

You know my name

Wanna get with me

Step up your game

MYEISHA dances, but can't hit the "right shoulder move." She notices that the CORONER cuts the record every time she gets to that move. She battles CORONER with the "right shoulder move" for control of the turntables trying to stop the him/her from cutting the record then letting it play. MYEISHA wins this battle.

5.

DJ/BEATBOXER samples a series of "Fours." MYEISHA dances the "scalp move" as the CORONER "cuts up" the following

CORONER   The entrance to gunshot wound number four is on the left posterior side of the head.

This is a typical distant gunshot wound entrance.

The course of the projectile is through the scalp and exiting the right posterior side of the scalp. The projectile does not enter or fracture the cranium, and the course is only through the scalp.

The exit on the right posterior scalp is a half inch irregular stellate hole without abrasion. This is a non-fatal distant gunshot wound perforating the scalp only.

MYEISHA Hold up...!

DJ/BEATBOXER samples "wait a minute, let me put some..."

I know he/she did not just say only through the scalp

I know she did not just say only talkin bout my scalp!

She must not realize that the only place my hair grows is on that scalp.

You know what

I'm not even gonna get into the whole Black women and their hair conversation right now

Not with a coroner anyhow

(Reluctant beat)

All I'm gon' say is Sarah Breedlove

Aka Madam CJ Walker

Aka first self-made American woman millionaire

Built on Black hair care

(To CORONER)

You hear!

(Beat)

Hot Iron burns on your forehead, scars your neck
Highlights, low-lights, frostin, tintin
Sleepin' sittin' up so your new style don't get wrecked
Kitchen sink perms
Combing through them naps
Baby hair pumpin'
Getting your dandruff scratched
Now I know some of my sistas you'all gone natural and I ain't hatin
All I'm sayin' is you don't wanna go there unless you are aware of the hair

Sample: LL's: Around The Way Girl. Bout CORONER's comment

Only through the scalp

Lemme give you Mr./Ms. Coroner some advice when addressing a Black woman's hair

The only time you wanna let only come out your mouth is if you're sayin

If only I could get my flip to flip as good as yours
If only I could get my goddess braids to rock as good as yours
If only I could get my wrap to drop as good as yours
If only I could get my micro braids to hold as good as yours

If only I could get my streaks to blend as good as yours
If only I could get my bob to hold as good as yours
If only I could get my Farrah Fawcett Feather to layer
as good as yours
If only I could get my quick weave to blend as good as
yours

Only through the scalp

And since I'm handing out advice
Let me give the men a little slice
You know me
I'm-a be nice
Brothas should already be aware of this fact
But if you ain't a brotha and you like your coffee black
Here's a little insight to help you with your mack

Do not touch the hair
Permed, relaxed, crimped, slicked, braided, dreaded or
fro
Please
Just let the hair go

Do not grab the hair
Do not stroke the hair
Do not caress the hair
Do not clutch the hair
Do not fondle the hair
Do not fiddle with the hair
Do not twiddle with the hair

Do not absentmindedly twirl the hair or swirl the hair
or curl the hair
Do not pensively seize the hair
Do not passionately grip the hair
Do not attempt to run your fingers through the hair
Do not kiss the hair
Do not lick the hair

Just

Did I make it clear
Hands off the hair

But if you care to get near the hair then be aware of
when hair's just been done
When sista's just come from Ebony Crest, Shear
Elegance or Miss Ellison
Make it very clear that you see the hair you feel the hair
And if allowed to
you would stroke the hair
you would caress the hair
you would clutch the hair
you would grab the hair
you would fondle fiddle twiddle and twirl the hair

I know it's not fair
But hey, hair's not fair
So if you really care
Do not touch the hair

And, oh yeah, when you see a sista goin like this

(Patting hair)

Don't be phased

Ain't nothin' wrong with her, she's only scratchin' her scalp through her braids

(Facetiously - bout the Coroner)

I know she/he did not say only through the scalp

Only through the scalp.

MYEISHA dances, but can't hit the "scalp move". She notices that the CORONER cuts the record every time she gets to that move. She battles CORONER with the "scalp move" for control of the turntables trying to stop the him/her from cutting the record then letting it play.

MYEISHA wins this battle

6.

DJ/BEATBOXER samples a series of "Fives". MYEISHA dances the "lower back move" as the CORONER "cuts up" the following

CORONER The entrance to gunshot number five is located on the central lower back.

The course of the of the projectile is through the skin and soft tissue of the left lower back and exiting the left anterior lateral hip.

This is a non-fatal gunshot wound to the left lower back.

MYEISHA I was in a video

Nah, fo' real

I was in a video

I was in this video

It was even on TV

Okay, so it was just like on channel 23

Exclusively local to the IE

Okay see, this emcee from Mo-Val got signed by Empire Records

Local label, think his name was MC D-Lo

And they about to release his first single and they 'bout to shoot the video

So me Shy and Toni are at Club Metro lettin ourselves go

This kid sees us, says he's shootin a video

Sees us doin our old routine

Not even the new one you just seen

Says he's lookin for some females to represent for the IE

So naturally, you know... Toni, Shy and me

(Like the Kid would say)

"You guys heard of Empire Records, right"

No

But we still show up for the shoot

Shoot, we just down to get our groove on

They were for real, had a director, a crew an everything

So on 'action' we did our thing

Okay, so you probably won't recognize us, you know

I thought they were serious

But when I saw the video all they showed was the angle on the gluteus

I'm mean I like my posterior, but I like my face too

I think they showed it once on B-E-T Un-cut

But in the final cut you don't-see-me

Least not from any angle where you could see me

All they showed was what me, Shy and Toni called the 'ho shot'

All bottom no top

Okay, so this is how Empire Records shot me.

Giving audience the B-E-T Uncut - angle on the posterior shot. Smirk on her face turns to disappointment to anger to sadness.

MYEISHA dances, but can't hit the "lower back move". She notices that the CORONER cuts the record every time she gets to that move. She battles CORONER with the "lower back move" for control of the turntables trying to

stop the him/her from cutting the record then letting it play.

MYEISHA wins this battle.

7.

DJ/BEATBOXER samples a series of "sixes". MYEISHA dances "fractured femur move" as the CORONER "cuts up" the following

CORONER The entrance to gunshot wound number six is located on the left thigh. The course of the projectile is through the skin and soft tissue of the left thigh, perforating, fracturing and fragmenting the left femur.

This is a non-fatal, however, serious gunshot wound to the left thigh, fracturing the left femur.

MYEISHA My cousin died once, well, almost died

No, not Toni, my cousin Freddie

Well he kind-a died

Okay, so if you know me and you know I gots sports skills

When it came to Freddie, sports kills

He's un-cordinated like-a-mug I mean like-a-mug

So when I heard he broke his leg I was like

Yeah

And?

Of course he broke his leg, it's Fred that's what he does

You know how you got that one cousin who always gets hurt

You could be playin tag, hide and seek, jump rope or diggin in the dirt

(Makes 'we made that game up' face)

You know you played diggin in the dirt

No matter what though

Guaranteed ... Freddie was gonna get hurt

Dropped a brick on his head ... that was funny

That one bled

Broke his left arm twice,

Broke his right arm once

Ankles always sprained

Usually the left, but the right one too

Always something caught in his eyes, even thought he
wore glasses

Over a hundred stitches, no lie

Had to sleep on the bottom bunk cause he would fall
out the bed

That was Fred

So then he gets hurt and starts cryin

We're like like "shhh, come on man, you act like you
dyin or somethin

Thing was

If one of our aunties heard Freddie's boo-hoo our game
was through

Toni used to get so mad at him she didn't know what to
do

(As TONI in the moment)

Damn Fred, shut up!

You act like a little girl

Long   as   there   was   no   blood   flow   though
Freddie was usually good to go

So
They take him to Kaiser --

Oh wait, let me break down the break
This fool goes out to Devil's Canyon out by Cal State
Rollin on a Mo-ped, a Mo-ped
That's a motorcycle that you pedal
So full speed ahead goes Fred
Crashes the Mo-ped

They take him to Kaiser Fontana
Soon's I find out I am on my way to the hospital
To have some fun
Get my *bag* on

When I get there he's like
"They just wanna keep me overnight then I'm-a go home"
Next day I'm learning about Fat Embolism Syndrome And
Freddie's not at home

He's in a coma
It was induced
That's how it was introduced

Doctors explained it this way
Fat embolism syndrome is a symptom complex of acute respiratory failure after long-bone fractures. It is thought to be caused by deposition of embolic fat within the pulmonary capillaries, resulting in a capillary leak within the lung. The source of the embolic fat appears to be marrow fat.

Freddie broke his Femur
The fat was headed to his lungs
Got stuck in his throat

So he's put into an *induced* coma for two weeks
Cause he was too weak to breathe or speak
Two weeks
Too weak to even eat
Like he was dead
In a hospital bed
They said
Told us it was good for him to hear familiar voices
So I showed up just about every day
Aunt Dee moved in to Kaiser Permanente
Permanently

My aunt Dee, Freddie's mom, had always been the auntie with faith
You know, the religious aunt who made sure you prayed in you car 'fore a long ride
Or dropped a "stay on the Lord's side" if she thought you were starting to backslide

Aunt Dee moved into the I-C-U
I-Kid-you not

Prayin my cousin back to this side
Sayin
"This coma ain't nothing but a comma in my son's life story"

After sixteen days Freddie woke up in a haze
First thing he says is
Cuz, I went to New York City
And I'm thinkin,
Not pretty
Shame
The Fat Emboli got his brain
How sad
And he's gettin mad
Cause nobody's believin' his New York City dream
Starts to scream about the weather, what he ate, where
he went, cash he spent

Talkin' bout he was

[Sample: Uptown Baby Uptown Baby]

Talkin bout he was in

[Sample: Brooklyn's in the house]

Talkin bout he was in

[Sample: Strong Island]

Talkin bout he was in

[Sample: South Bronx, the South-South Bronx]

Talkin bout he was in

[Sample: The Bridge]

*DJ/BEATBOXER goes into a serious South Bronx/The
Bridge mix*
I'm like, fool, you were right here in
(singing) Fontana baby Fontana baby

With yo' mama baby yo' mama baby

(spoken) Freddie didn't think that was too funny

Anyways who knows

Maybe Freddie did go to New York city

I sure hope aunt Dee has some of her prayer power left over for me

(Beat)

I ain't never been to New York

MYEISHA dances, hits the "fractured femur move". She notices that the CORONER cuts the record every time she gets to that move. She battles CORONER with the "fractured femur move" for control of the turntables trying to stop the him/her from cutting the record then letting it play.

MYEISHA wins this battle.

8.

MYEISHA remains frozen in position from last scene while DJ/BEATBOXER samples a series of "sevens". MYEISHA dances "lower back move" as the CORONER "cuts up" the following

CORONER The entrance of gunshot number 7 is located on the right middle back.

The course of the projectile is through the subcutaneous tissue of the right central back. The bullet did not enter the chest.

This is a non-fatal gunshot wound to the chest.

(At the tattoo spot with TONI.)

MYEISHA "Toni, you sure 'bout this spot?"

Yeah girl, this is where I got mine done and you know mine's hot

Yeah, I'm here for a tat

My cousin tells me you got skills

You got a problem with that

My lower back

Nefertiti

Queen

Black

Here, Toni where's the one you drew ?

(Shows Tattoo Artist TONI's Nefertiti drawing)

My cousin got skills, huh?

You told me forty not sixty-five Let's go What ?

(To Toni) That's all I got

Let me get twenty-five I'll pay you back
I know I ain't got no job
You don't have to bust me out

Just do me this favor I'll get you back Just like I got yo'
back last month Don't front

Aw'rite let's see what you can do

(Positions herself in tattoo chair)

Hold up, wait Is it gonna hurt?
Do pigs like dirt, that's funny But fo' real though
Tiny pieces of fire tappin' your skin But then-- Numb,
that'll work
Aw'rite
Begin

She was powerful, beautiful and smart like me
Her name means "The beautiful woman has come" I'm
here!
I'm puttin' her there cause only kings get to see the
queen Know what I mean
Trust me, it'll be the last time you see her

Two hours?!

I told uncle Darnell I was thinkin 'bout gettin'a tattoo
I can be just like you He says:
First of all ain't nobody gon see it dark as you are
Second, a tattoo ain't nothin but a scar

You can get a scar if you want
From me
For free
The pain'll be the same
Just won't take as long
Then he starts going into one of his his "black-outs"

(Imitating Uncle DARNELL)

You would-a never made it as no slave

It'll be a hundred degrees ... IE heat
And if I forget and say "Man, it is hot"
You would-a never made it as no slave
"This ain't nothin' but dry heat
Down South they got that humid heat plus massa wasn't givin you much to eat"

I get me some new tennis shoes
"You would-a never made it as a slave
They didn't even have shoes
You'd just be steppin with your bare feet on the hard concrete"
He always tried to throw in some lame hip hop to prove he was cool Even when I did something right, like help him move our couch
"You would-a never made it as no slave"
"Don't you know that once you let 'em know how hard you could work That's how hard you would work"
So I dropped the couch

MYEISHA dances, hits the "lower back move." She notices that the CORONER cuts the record every time she gets to that move.

She battles CORONER with the "lower back move" for control of the turntables trying to stop the him/her from cutting the record then letting it play. MYEISHA wins this battle

9.

DJ/BEATBOXER samples a series of "eights." MYEISHA dances the "lower back move" as the CORONER "cuts" up the following

CORONER The entrance to gunshot number eight is located on the right lower back.

The course of thee projectile is throught the skin and soft tissue of the right lower back and perforating and fracturing the third lumbar vertebra.

This is a non-fatal gunshot wound to the right lower back.

MYEISHA

They found my "C" in junior high

(Showing lower back)

See? Here's how

There was a screening one day that seemed to be pretty benign

They drew a line we stood in line they took a look at our spine

A few days later came a letter saying I needed further testing

After X-rays the doctor says he didn't like the way my spine was resting

The diagnosis... scoliosis a lower "C" curve

Not like Becca who had a "S" - hers was an internal swerve

Told I had to wear a plastic brace for two years in my case

This thing went all the way from my chest down to my
waist

I'd have to be encased in this brace to prevent improper
alignment

Since I didn't embrace the exercises the doctor gave me
as my assignment

*MYEISHA demonstrates exercise using chair, as DJ/
BEATBOXER narrates instructions in instructionally-
monotone voice*

DJ/BEATBOXER This exercise aims to align the spine
and activate under-used muscles. Stand next to an
elevated bench so that the edge of the bench is near
your hip. The leg on the same side as the thoracic
concavity should be against the bench. Lean to the
side over the bench and bring up your leg to form a
straight line with your body. The foot should point up.
The shoulder and the hip that are on the same side as
the rib hump should be slightly back. The palm on the
same arm should face up. Your other arm should push
against the surface of the bench, so that the shoulder
above the thoracic concavity is as high as possible.
Try to lengthen your neck as far as you can, against
in the direction of your thoracic curve. Also try to
reach as far as you can with the raised leg. Feel your
spine straightening and lengthening. Breathe into the
thoracic concavity while maintaining this position.
Feel the thoracic concavity getting wider and larger.
Continue breathing slowly deeper and deeper.

MYEISHA Since I didn't embrace the exercises the
doctor gave me as my assignment

I'd have to be encased in this brace to prevent improper
alignmen

Told I was gonna have to wear it for two years straight, eighth grade and ninth

The first year wasn't too bad, but the second we were gonna have a fight

Ninth grade – first year of high school

Now you know that was not cool

I wasn't 'bout to show up as a freshman looking like a fresh fool

Like some kind-a geek

Like some kind-a freek

All grotesque

A whole year-an'-a-half 'fore I got my second base chest

So I was like, forget it, I figured I might as well just

Take the chance take the risk

I mean the worst thing that could happen to me, I guess, is that I'd have some back pain when I got old, like 56

Worst thing… I guess… back pain at 56

MYEISHA dances, hits the "lower back move". She notices that the CORONER cuts the record every time she gets to that move. She battles CORONER with the "lower back move" for control of the turntables trying to stop the him/her from cutting the record then letting it play

MYEISHA wins this battle.

10.

DJ/BEATBOXER samples a series of "Nines" MYEISHA dances "left breast move" as the CORONER "cuts up" the following

CORONER The entrance to gunshot number nine is through the left breast. The wound is located five inches to the left of the anterior midline and fourteen inches down from the top of the head. This is a typical distant gunshot wound entrance.

The course of the projectile is through the soft tissue of the left breast, through the anterior chest wall and exiting below the right breast.

The exit to gunshot wound six is located below the right breast. This is a non-fatal gunshot wound perforating the left breast.

MYEISHA If you know me you know I wasn't

One of the early bloomers like my cousin

'Til I was like sixteen it seemed like "A" was gonna be the only letter on my bra ever

Clever Ricky and his friends got to callin' me "Manchester"

Wanna know what I called their sorry behinds

Never mind

But then I turned sixteen
And bam

I mean boom!
I mean pow!
I mean wow!

I got mine

(Chest pop move from "Dance of the Dozens")

Second base all in yo' face

Now it wasn't like I was easy... or fast or loose

But that don't mean I didn't let loose when I let loose

I guess if I wanted to I could tell you that I'm a virgin

But that wouldn't be the honest version

Waited 'til I was sixteen though

I didn't know if we were even doin' it right

No lights

Dontrey kept talkin' 'bout how the time was right

How he was the last of his boys in line

How that wasn't right

Thing was, Dontrey was *foine*

And once we did it we did it all night long *(Curtis Blow style) till the break-a-dawn*

Well, at least that's Dontrey's version

But let's just say that dawn came with a quickness-can I get a witness...

That night

But

It was still alright

It was still alright

(Back in the moment)

Mouth was slightly open...

eyes were closed...

breathing shallow...

lips quivering...
body shaking.
Dontrey liked my lips he dug my hips, but yes, he loved
my chest
Confessed my chest was the best
Good guess
He was a breast man
And at sixteen, like I said, I had the best man
Forget the rest, come caress
Why settle for less
man

Just stop right there
Do not touch the hair

At sixteen stopped wondering found out for sure
At seventeen stopped accepting and started wanting
more
At eighteen declared myself a woman, grown... mature
At nineteen awaiting 20... knockin' on heaven's door
Awaiting twenty
A weight in twenty
I wait for twenty
At sixteen stopped wondering found out for sure
At seventeen stopped accepting and started wanting
more
At eighteen declared myself a woman, grown... mature
At nineteen awaiting 20... knockin' on heaven's door

At twenty a teenager no more... grown

I'm gon learn to moan
At twenty a teenager no more... grown
I'm gon' learn to moan
But sounds like twenty's getting out of reach
And I'm running out of time
Half-a-dozen on one hand six on the other, figure of speech
And I'm running out of rhyme
Seems like a crime
To waste all that I bring to the table
So why don't we agree to make this tale a fable
Let's agree to make this a fable
Seems like a crime
To waste all that I bring to the table
So why don't we agree to make this tale a fable

(Rappin' with DJ/Beatboxer as backup)

Once upon a time in the Inland Empire
There lived a young girl wanted to spit fire
There lived a young girl wanted to spit fire
There live a young girl --

Why don't we agree to make this tale a fable
Then if you're able, if you can
If it's not too much to ask

When they finish singing your happy 19th birthday
before you make your wish and blow
Put a candle on your cake for me to add to the glow
Close your eyes and wish that what you're seeing ain't

nothin' but a dream-fable

And I'm gonna wake up nineteen at your birthday table

Close your eyes and wish that what you're seeing ain't nothin' but a dream-fable

And I'm gonna wake up nineteen at your birthday table

Put another candle on to add to the glow

Now make your wish and blow

OFFICER GARLAND Miller's mouth was slightly open, her eyes were closed, her breathing appeared shallow, her lips were quivering, her body was shaking, and a white substance was accumulating around the sides of her mouth.

MYEISHA At nineteen...

Knockin' on heaven's door.

MYEISHA dances, hits the "left breast move". She notices that the CORONER cuts the record every time she gets to that move. She battles CORONER with the "left breast move" for control of the turntables trying to stop the him/her from cutting the record then letting it play.

MYEISHA wins this battle

11.

DJ/BEATBOXER samples series of "tens." MYEISHA does the "upper left forehead" move.

CORONER The entrance to gunshot number ten is located on the left upper forehead. This is a typical distant gunshot wound entrance.

The course of the projectile is through the skin of the forehead, entering the cranium through the left frontal bone, through the left and right frontal lobes of the brain, through the right orbit perforating and rupturing the right ocular globe and exiting the right orbit.

The direction of the projectile is back-to-front, left-to-right and downward 45 degrees. This is a fatal distant gunshot wound to the head.

MYEISHA battles CORONER for control of the turntables trying to stop the him/her from cutting the record then letting it play.

The CORONER wins this battle

12.

DJ/BEATBOXER samples series of "elevens." MYEISHA does the "left ear move"

CORONER The entrance of gunshot wound number eleven is above and behind the left ear on the left side of the head. This is a typical distant gunshot wound entrance.

The course of the projectile is through the scalp, entering the cranium through the left occipital bone, perforating the left cerebellum, perforating the pons of the brain stem and penetrating into the anterior base of the cranium.

This is a *fatal* distant gunshot wound to the head.

13.

DJ/BEATBOXER samples series of "twelves." MYEISHA does the "right central back" move.

CORONER The entrance to gunshot number twelve is located on the right central back. This is a typical distant gunshot wound entrance.

The direction of the projectile is back-to-front, left-to-right and slightly upward three degrees.

This is a fatal distant gunshot wound to the chest perforating the right lung.

MYEISHA holds headphones to left ear, as if in recording studio

MYEISHA *(Rapping)* One-to-the-chest

One-to-the-arm

One-to-the-leg

One-to-the-neck

One-to-the-dome

One-to-the-dome

One-to-the-dome

One-to-the-back

One-to-the back

One-to-the-back

One-to-the-back

One-to-the-back

I bet you ain't seen no female MC who's been shot as many times as me

Not since Supersonic has a female MC from the west
put it down with the best
You know, one of the J's from JJ Fad lives in the IE
For a minute I was thinkin' of rappin' in Pig Latin
But that ain't hap'nin
This is the key right here
It's been a year since they shot Biggie
Since Tupac was killed it's been two
It just makes sense that this should happen to me now
I gotta live
I'll be the first female MC ever
Too clever
Before me MCs only been shot a couple times
And lived
I got a dozen and I still be spittin rhymes
You can't stop me this is my time to shine

One-to-the-chest
One-to-the-arm
One-to-the-leg
One-to-the-neck

One-to-the-dome
One-to-the-dome
One-to-the-dome

One-to-the-back
One-to-the-back
One-to-the-back

> One-to-the-back
>
> One-to-the-back

DJ/BEATBOXER The average person can hold their breath for sixty to ninety seconds

> The lungs take in oxygen enriched air first and gets rid of carbon dioxide second
>
> The average person breathes in and out 15 to 25 times every 60 seconds
>
> Breath enters through the nose and mouth first, phrynx and larnyx second

MYEISHA exhales.

> There are two phases to the process of breathing
>
> Inspiration happens first
>
> Expiration happens second

MYEISHA "INSPIRES" and "EXPIRES" 25 times. DJ/ BEATBOXER speaks the following on her breaths. Breaths should be taken meditatively, gradually slowing, then coming to stop.

> Creativity
>
> Release
>
> Insight
>
> Conclusion
>
> Inventiveness
>
> Completion
>
> Ingenuity
>
> Closure
>
> Imagination
>
> Exhalation

Revelation
Cessation
Stimulation
Departure
Arousal
Eradication
Muse
Expelled
Motivation
Termination

Vision
Discontinuance
Illumination
Extinction
Elevation
Execution
Enthusiasm
Closure
Invigoration
Obliteration

Exuberance
Collapse
Excitement
Finale
Fervor
Finish
Elation

Termination

Vivification

Death

Awakening

Passing

Uplift

Exit

Rapture

Deceased

Alpha

Omega

Beginning

MYEISHA *(Rushing to get to bed. In one breath)* Now I lay me down to sleep

I pray the Lord my soul to keep

If I should die before I wake

I pray the Lord my soul to take

Bless mommy and daddy, Shy, Freddie, aunt Dee and my cousin Toni

This is Myeisha

You know me.

DJ/BEATBOXER Ending

MYEISHA STOPS BREATHING. The CORONER wins the battle, "celebrates" by mixing/repeating the following while MYEISHA dances the "12 mortal moves "to Otis Redding's White Christmas.

CORONER Right lung weighed 270 grams

Left lung weighed 325 grams

Liver weighed 975 grams

Spleen weighed 100 grams

Kidneys weighed 100 grams each

Brain weighed 1,025 grams

Heart weighed 275 grams and was smooth and glistening

MYEISHA finishes her dance then gets back into th white Nissan Sentra.

MYEISHA Ever have one of those dreams
   Where nothing comes out when you try to scream.

She falls into her final sleep.

THE END.

"A salutary interruption to the anesthetic pleasures that theatre so often provides, *Dreamscape* refuses the compact between stage and audience that promises escape. Instead, it insists on reckoning. *Dreamscape* is less a dramatization than a poem as autopsy, a careful examination of a future stolen before it had the chance to harden into memory.

One leaves the theatre not soothed or satisfied but altered—carrying anger, grief, and, most insistently, a name that will not loosen its grip.

The production frames Miller's life and death as a modern fable, one that demands repetition as an ethical act. Say her name. Say it again.

Dreamscape asks what it means when even that final refuge is violated. What happens when the body opens its mouth to scream and nothing comes out—when judgment, sentencing, and execution collapse into a single, irreversible moment?

Hip-hop and rap glide through the piece, touching on the frivolities of star signs and flirtation, all the while threading us toward an ending that cannot be revised. The effect confronts the relentless vulnerability of Black bodies and the grinding pursuit of justice that follows their destruction.

What emerges most forcefully is a bracing, almost accusatory reminder of what it means to be marked as other – not as an abstract sociological category, but as a lived, daily condition that seeps into posture, speech, and self-conception. The work insists that such treatment is never neutral, never merely symbolic; it exacts a toll that accrues over time, charging interest on every slight, exclusion, and misrecognition. To inhabit a life circumscribed by otherness, the piece suggests, is to pay continually for one's existence, in vigilance, in compromise, in the quiet erosion of possibility. That this reminder arrives now only sharpens its resonance: the theater here becomes both mirror and ledger, reckoning with the costs we ask some bodies to bear so that others may remain comfortably unexamined."

– Tony Marinelli, theatrebeyondbroadway.com

More plays to perform:

Noor by Azma Dar
ISBN 978-1-912430-72-7 £9.99
Humane by Polly Creed
ISBN 978-1-912430-57-4 £9.99
Wollstonecraft Live! by Kaethe Fine
ISBN 978-1-912430-61-1 £11.99
Diary of a Hounslow Girl by Ambreen Razia
ISBN 978-0-9536757-9-1 £8.99
Harvest by Manjula Padmanabhan
ISBN 978-0-9536757-7-7 £9.99
Mistaken: Annie Besant in India by Rukhsana
Ahmad ISBN 978-0-9551566-9-4 £7.99
Penetration by Carolyn Lloyd-Davies
ISBN 978-1-912430-63-5 £9.99
The Curious Lives of Shakespeare and Cervantes by Asa
Palomera ISBN 978-1-911501-13-8 £9.99
The Marvellous Adventures of Mary Seacole by Cleo
Sylvestre ISBN 978-1-912430-59-8 £8.99
Three Mothers by Matilda Velevitch
ISBN 978-1-912430-35-2 £9.99

For collections of plays see:

www.aurorametro.com